Tax Time Account
Direct Mail Pilot
Evaluation

Tax Time Account Direct Mail Pilot Evaluation

This document is based on a report authored by Caroline Ratcliffe and Signe-Mary McKernan of the Urban Institute. The report was completed by the Urban Institute under a contract with the U.S. Department of the Treasury, Order Number GS-23F-8198H/ T09BPA017, with funds authorized by the U.S. Department of the Treasury.

This report was completed pursuant to the Improving Access to Mainstream Financial Services Act of 2010 (Title XII of the Dodd-Frank Wall Street Reform and Consumer Protection Act).

Table of Contents

Tax Time Account Direct Mail Pilot Evaluation

Executive Summary

Electronic delivery of tax refunds through direct deposit to bank accounts is used by most upper-income families, but has so far eluded many low- and moderate-income families. One of the benefits of electronic delivery versus paper checks is lower administrative cost for the federal government—roughly one-tenth the cost of a paper check. Beyond this, electronic delivery provides tax filers faster, safer and more reliable access to tax refunds, and can improve low- and moderate-income tax filers' access to mainstream financial services, a goal of Title XII of the Dodd-Frank Wall Street Reform and Consumer Protection Act.

Many low- and moderate-income working families receive a sizable federal tax refund, primarily through refundable tax credits such as the earned income tax credit (EITC). Many families opt to receive a check or turn to alternative financial services to access their refunds or cash their refund checks, which may undermine financial access and asset-building goals. At least 17 million U.S. adults are unbanked and about 43 million are underbanked (FDIC 2009);[1] access to mainstream financial services would bring these adults federally insured accounts to build savings, cash checks, pay bills, and avoid expensive alternative financial services.

The U.S. Department of the Treasury's pilot program delivered tax refunds electronically and increased access to the mainstream financial sector for a small sample of the low- and moderate-income population. Given the importance of properly designing an account for its target consumer, the Tax Time Account pilot was designed to evaluate card features and messaging for low- and moderate-income unbanked tax filers. The results of the pilot will help ensure that the potential effects of certain account design features are well understood before evaluating future options that could, for example, integrate an account option into the tax-filing and refund process.

Specifically, the pilot offered low- and moderate-income tax filers a safe, low-cost account for the electronic delivery of their federal tax refunds. The account can continue to be used for multiple purposes, including ongoing direct deposit of earnings and cash loading, point-of-sale transactions, safe storage of funds, ATM withdrawal, and bill payment. The U.S. Department of the Treasury selected Bonneville Bank as the financial agent for the Tax Time Account pilot. Bonneville Bank selected Green Dot to provide card processing services for the Visa branded card. The card may be used at any point-of-sale terminal that accepts the Visa card world-wide.

Electronic delivery of tax refund payments may have many benefits for the government and taxpayers. Tax refund payments are made once a year and many are for significant dollar amounts. However, simply converting a once-a-year check payment to a once-a-year plastic card may not

---

[1] Unbanked adults have no checking or savings account. Underbanked adults have a checking or savings account but rely on alternative financial services such as (nonbank) check-cashing services, refund anticipation loans, payday loans, pawn shops, money orders, and rent-to-own agreements.
The FDIC study can be found at http://www.economicinclusion.gov/household_survey.html

provide savings for the government. The expense of providing a taxpayer with a plastic card annually for this singular purpose would be greater than disbursing a payment via a paper check.

Instead, Treasury is exploring approaches that would provide low- and moderate-income tax filers the ability to choose a financial account that could be used for deposit of their tax refunds, and also function as an ongoing financial account for depositing other income, paying bills, making in-person and online purchases, and withdrawing cash, among other purposes. For two reasons, this approach could be more economical than a paper check—for the taxpayer as well as for the government. First, recipients would be more likely to retain a financial account that can be used in an ongoing way, making it possible to send them electronic refunds in future years. Second, the economics of an ongoing account appear to be more viable for financial providers, potentially making it possible to furnish the account at a low or no cost to consumers if done on a wide scale.

Under the pilot, roughly 800,000 individuals were randomly selected from a population of more than 8 million adults who were likely to be low- and moderate-income (under $35,000 in household income) and live in an unbanked or underbanked household.[2] The 808,099 people were then randomly assigned to one of eight treatment groups. Pilot participants in each treatment group were mailed an offer to sign up for the *MyAccountCard*. The eight treatment groups differ along three dimensions: (1) no monthly fee versus low monthly fee ($4.95), (2) linked savings account versus no linked savings account, and (3) convenience-focused messaging versus safety-focused messaging. Based on these three categories, the eight treatment groups are as follows:

Group	Monthly Fee	Savings Account	Message
Treatment 1	No fee	Yes	Safety
Treatment 2	No fee	Yes	Convenience
Treatment 3	No fee	No	Safety
Treatment 4	No fee	No	Convenience
Treatment 5	Fee	Yes	Safety
Treatment 6	Fee	Yes	Convenience
Treatment 7	Fee	No	Safety
Treatment 8	Fee	No	Convenience

The pilot evaluation measures the impact of the different prepaid card offers on the *MyAccountCard* sign-up rate, subsequent card use, and accumulated account balances. For example, people assigned to receive a card with no monthly maintenance fee are compared with those who received a card offer with a monthly maintenance fee to gauge the impact of the fee on take-up and use. Similarly, people who received a card offer without a linked savings account (or safety messaging) are compared with those who are offered a savings account (or convenience messaging).

Pilot participants were on average 46 years old and almost evenly split between males/females and white/nonwhite participants. All participants had estimated annual household incomes below

_____
[2] These adults were identified using commercially available data from Experian Marketing Solutions Inc.

$35,000, with roughly a third in each of three income categories (<$15,000, $15,000–$24,999, and $25,000–$34,999). The participants' average underbanked score of 5 falls in the middle of the 1–9 range, where 1 indicates households most likely to be unbanked/underbanked and successively higher values indicate a lower likelihood of being unbanked/underbanked.[3]

Overall, 1,967 people (0.3 percent) who received a *MyAccountCard* offer applied for this prepaid card, of which 1,933 people (98.3 percent) were issued the card. This 0.3 percent take-up is in the 0.3 percent to 0.8 percent range of credit card direct mail take-up rates in recent years (Kiviat 2010; Woosley 2007). Although credit cards and prepaid cards are different products, the credit card take-up rates provide a benchmark for the take-up rate of card products offered through direct mail. Importantly, the card take-up rate was significantly higher for people who were most likely in unbanked households. Pilot participants identified as most likely to be unbanked had a take-up rate of 0.8 percent. This take-up rate, which is nearly three times higher than the take-up rate for the full pilot population, is at the higher end of the expected range and exceeds recent first quarter take-up rates. Only a subset of cardholders directly deposited their tax refunds into the card accounts. Sixteen percent of all cardholders and 48 percent of active cardholders did so. The analyses show that the timing of the card offer was also important for take-up—the findings indicate that earlier is better. People mailed the offer in mid-January were 85 percent more likely to apply for the card than those mailed the offer in early February. This provides helpful direction for any future efforts and suggests that information about the prepaid card program should be distributed and made available before the tax-filing season begins.

Some elements of the pilot likely lowered the take-up rate. These elements include timing of the offer letters, quality of the Experian mailing list (addresses and target characteristics), a multistep process for receiving one's tax refund into the account, and absence of a comprehensive informational "surround sound" campaign.[4] Also, the *MyAccountCard* cannot be used to pay tax preparation fees, which likely reduced its usefulness for low- and moderate-income tax filers that use paid tax preparers and who did not have the $150–$400 tax preparation fee upfront.[5] While some of these items were apparent at the start of the pilot, they were accepted as part of its design, but would be rectified in any future pilot or program focused on enhancing take-up of a card product.

The pilot was designed to measure the effect of different aspects of card offers on take-up, not overall card take-up. Any future efforts would likely offer the card through a different mechanism— likely directly in the tax filing and refund process rather than through the direct mail offer used for

---

[3] The household likelihood of being unbanked or underbanked is a variable constructed by Experian Marketing Solutions Inc. and is based on a statistical model that produces an underbanked score, where values between 1 and 9 identify households likely to be unbanked or underbanked.

[4] An informational surround sound campaign is an effort to use earned and paid media, community partners, and population relevant organizations to make the public receiving the offer aware of its existence and the process by which to take action.

[5] Fees for tax preparation services vary by provider. Average fees at H&R Block and Jackson Hewitt ranged between $185 and $210 in 2010 (Perez 2010), but have been found to reach more than $400 (Wu and Fox 2011).

the pilot. The results of the pilot provide helpful data about the potential effects of certain card design features to inform future potential options, including those that would integrate card offers in the tax filing and refund process.

One of the tested features—card cost—stands out as influencing the behavior of pilot participants in a significant and consistent way. Charging a $4.95 monthly maintenance fee (versus no monthly maintenance fee) decreased *MyAccountCard* applications and issuance by 42 and 43 percent, respectively. The estimated own-price elasticity of demand implies that a 10 percent increase in the monthly cost of the *MyAccountCard* reduces card applications and issuance by 2.6 percent. Analyses of different subpopulations find that people in households likely to be unbanked are somewhat less sensitive to the price of the card.[6] Unbanked households may be more likely to pay a monthly fee for the prepaid cards because they have fewer banking options.

Card use also decreased with the $4.95 monthly maintenance fee. The likelihood of using the card within the first six months of the pilot was 47 percent lower for people offered a card with the monthly fee. Measures of longer-term card use are also lower among those who face the monthly fee. People offered a card with the $4.95 monthly fee were 55 percent less likely to actively use their *MyAccountCard* six months after the pilot was launched and 52 percent less likely to directly deposit a tax refund into their accounts.

Outcomes for pilot participants offered and not offered the linked savings account are similar. Adults offered the linked savings account (versus not offered the linked savings account) were not significantly more likely to apply for or be issued a *MyAccountCard,* nor did they have higher account balances. The savings account feature tested in the pilot required additional cardholder action to activate the savings account (i.e., online activation) and deposits could not be made directly into the savings account (i.e., only transfers from the transaction account were allowed); different implementation could have produced different results. Product messaging (safety versus convenience) did not significantly influence pilot participant behavior.

The results of the Tax Time Account direct mail pilot offer lessons for moving forward with a similar account offer by Treasury. The pilot established proof of concept for offering a card account in conjunction with tax time. Offering and issuing cards, and delivering tax refunds to those accounts, proved feasible for Treasury operationally. In addition, the pilot established that there is a market and a demand for such a product. That direct mail take-up rates are, in absolute terms, low, but not appreciably different from similar direct mail efforts, serves primarily to underscore the importance of Treasury delivering the card with both different enrollment methods and in a different marketing context at scale. Streamlining the card's delivery, for example, by offering the card directly in the tax filing and refund process, would reduce barriers to application and likely encourage more take-up. Publicizing such a card broadly and before tax season begins should increase filers' familiarity with the product, and thus, its take-up and use.

---

[6] These results are only marginally statistically significant (at the 10 percent level).

This pilot produced a set of valuable lessons that could inform any potential future use of the tax refund delivery process as a means to reduce paper checks and to help expand access to mainstream financial products. Tests focusing on the card's features suggest that individuals are price sensitive with respect to monthly fees, and that linked savings accounts (at least as designed in this pilot) were not perceived as valuable. Implications for future efforts suggest that Treasury direct its efforts primarily toward offering an account with a monthly fee as low as possible (zero if possible), even at the expense of additional card features such as a savings account.

In sum, the federal government's creation of an option for tax filers to receive refunds directly onto a low-cost, account-linked card, as tested in this pilot, is a concept with promise. Such a card can reduce costs to Treasury, by reducing the number of costly paper checks used to deliver refunds. And such considerations are only one dimension of the potential benefits. Such a product could also reduce low- and moderate-income tax filers' use of expensive alternative financial service outlets to cash their refund checks, as well as reduce the use of high-cost tax return options such as refund anticipation checks, especially if the product enables users to pay for tax preparation. And for those without a bank account, such a product could bring the benefits of access to mainstream financial services.

However, the pilot was not designed to measure the demand for an account-linked card or the costs of delivering such a card in a real-world setting. Thus, the net benefit of offering such a card cannot be determined by the pilot and hence is unknown.

Tax Time Account Direct Mail Pilot Evaluation

I. Introduction

Federal and state governments have increasingly made efforts to distribute benefits electronically, decreasing associated costs and improving access. In 2010, more than 90 federal, state, and local government-funded programs used prepaid cards to deliver benefits (Board of Governors 2011). Programs providing benefits electronically include the Supplemental Nutrition Assistance Program (SNAP, previously known as the Food Stamp Program); Temporary Assistance for Needy Families (TANF); Women, Infants, and Children (WIC); Social Security; and Supplemental Security Income (SSI). Electronic delivery of tax refunds through direct deposit to bank accounts is used by most middle and upper-income families, but has so far eluded many low- and moderate-income families. In addition to decreasing administrative costs and making access to refunds more reliable, electronic delivery of tax refunds for low- and moderate-income families could accomplish other important goals.

With direct deposit and an account, tax time could improve access to mainstream financial services, a goal of Title XII of the Dodd-Frank Wall Street Reform and Consumer Protection Act. Access to mainstream financial services provides federally insured accounts to build savings, cash checks, pay bills, avoid expensive alternative financial services, earn a credit rating, and enter a virtuous circle of asset accumulation that may eventually lead to saving for college, a down payment on a home, or a secure retirement. Yet at least 17 million U.S. adults in nearly 9 million households are unbanked and about 43 million adults are underbanked (FDIC 2009).[1] These disproportionately low- and moderate-income and minority Americans lack access to a safe financial account (FDIC 2009)—an important vehicle for saving and a precursor to asset building.

Many low- and moderate-income working families receive a sizable federal tax refund, primarily through refundable tax credits such as the earned income tax credit (EITC). To date, the federal government has largely not used tax refunds as an opportunity to help provide access to mainstream financial products. Instead, many families turn to alternative financial services to access their refunds, which may further undermine financial access and asset-building goals. These families are often faced with the cost of check-cashing fees or—if they are unable to wait for mailed checks or pay for tax preparation—fees associated with refund anticipation loans (RALs) or refund anticipation checks (RACs).[2] RALs or RACs have been used by about 20 million tax filers annually since 2005 and were used by half of EITC recipients with qualifying children in 2009 (Theodos et al. 2010). In the last several years, RAL use has been replaced by RAC use because most banks

---

[1] Unbanked adults have no checking or savings account. Underbanked adults have a checking or savings account but rely on alternative financial services such as (nonbank) check-cashing services, refund anticipation loans, payday loans, pawn shops, money orders, and rent-to-own agreements.

[2] RALs are bank loans borrowed against anticipated tax refunds (less tax preparation and RAL fees) that are obtained through tax preparers and tax preparer software. RALs enable tax filers to receive their refunds faster—the same day (for an extra charge) or in a few days, rather than a few weeks. Tax filers might expect to pay about $72 for a $1,500 RAL (Theodos et al. 2011). RACs provide tax refunds (less tax preparation and RAC fees) in the form of a paper check or debit card after the bank has opened a temporary bank account and the IRS has directly deposited the tax filer's refund into the account. Tax payers can expect to pay roughly $57 for a RAC (Theodos et al. 2011).

1

stopped offering RALs in 2011 when the IRS eliminated the debt indicator. The debt indicator, which indicated to the tax preparer whether the tax filer had federal debts that might reduce or eliminate his or her tax refund, was provided by the IRS to encourage electronic filing and direct deposit and was used by banks as a risk mitigation tool.[3]

The U.S. Department of the Treasury's (Treasury) Tax Time Account pilot program delivered tax refunds electronically, increases access to mainstream financial products, and provides a low-cost partial alternative to refund anticipation checks. It offered low- and moderate-income tax filers a safe, convenient, low-cost financial account for the electronic delivery of their federal tax returns. The account, issued by Bonneville Bank, provided by Green Dot, and branded by Visa can also be used for purchases anywhere that Visa is accepted. In addition the card can be used to receive paychecks by direct deposit, withdraw cash, pay bills, and build savings. However, the *MyAccountCard* cannot be used to pay tax preparation fees, thereby limiting the card's usefulness among low- and moderate-income tax filers who use paid tax preparers and do not have the $150–$400 upfront to pay for tax preparation services (which are often used because of complicated EITC tax forms).[4] RALs and RACs, for example, are often used by low-income tax filers who do not have means to pay their tax preparation fees (Barr and Dokko 2008; Theodos et al. 2010).[5]

The Tax Time Account pilot was designed to evaluate account features and messaging for low- and moderate-income unbanked tax filers. Treasury used randomization to offer variations of the *MyAccountCard* to assess which specific product features and marketing messages generated the greatest positive response from tax filers. The pilot was designed to measure the effect of different aspects of card offers on take-up, not overall card take-up. The results of the pilot will help ensure that the potential effects of certain account design features are well understood before evaluating future options that could, for example, integrate an account option into the tax-filing and refund process.

Broadly, the pilot evaluation empirically measures the effect of card features and messages on (1) take-up of the *MyAccountCard*, (2) receipt of tax refunds via direct deposit into the card account, and (3) card usage over time. The evaluation finds that charging a $4.95 monthly maintenance fee (versus no monthly maintenance fee) for the *MyAccountCard* reduced card applications, issuance, and transactional use by 40 to 55 percent. The linked savings account feature did not significantly increase card applications or use, nor is there evidence that it led to greater savings. Similarly, product messaging (safety versus convenience) did not significantly influence pilot participant behavior.

---

[3] The debt indicator was important to banks because the tax refund was used to secure and repay the RAL (Theodos et al. 2010, U.S. Government Accountability Office 2011). Besides the loss of the debt indicator, banks have also exited the RAL industry because of concerns about the stigma attached to RALs as well as directives from the Office of the Comptroller of the Currency (OCC) and the FDIC related to RAL safety and soundness, especially with the loss of the debt indicator.

[4] Fees for tax preparation services vary by provider. Average fees at H&R Block and Jackson Hewitt ranged between $185 and $210 in 2010 (Perez 2010), but these fees can reach upwards of $400 (Wu and Fox 2011).

[5] Barr and Dokko (2008) find nearly half of RAL and RAC users cite paying for tax preparation as an important reason for taking out the RAL or RAC, although Elliehausen (2005) finds it is not the primary reason.

The remainder of the report provides background on electronic government benefits, describes the pilot, data, measures, and analytical approach, and presents the pilot results, along with their implications for future efforts.

II. Background

Government has made huge strides in providing non-tax refund payments electronically. The 1996 Debt Collection Improvement Act required that most federal payments (except tax payments) be made electronically beginning in January 1999. As of December 2011, almost 90 percent of federal government benefit recipients are paid electronically (U.S. Department of the Treasury 2011). Electronic payments are safer and more reliable than paper checks. Every year, the Treasury Department has nearly 1.3 million problems with paper check payments (as described on Financial Management Service public website). Electronic payments are also less expensive than paper checks: it costs the U.S. government only 10 cents to issue an electronic payment but $1.02 to issue a paper check.[6]

A lack of a bank account is a key barrier to electronic payment for many recipients, although prepaid cards have been a common method for providing electronic payments to unbanked recipients. More than 90 government-funded programs use some form of prepaid card to deliver benefits, including SNAP, WIC, TANF, Social Security, and SSI. The SNAP program was a pioneer in providing electronic benefits. Electronic benefits transfer (EBT) cards were introduced in Pennsylvania in 1984 and adopted in all states by 2004 (Chakravorti and Lubasi 2006). In 2008, Treasury launched the Direct Express® MasterCard branded prepaid card as an option for unbanked federal benefit recipients, including Social Security and SSI recipients. The card can be used to receive benefits, pay bills, make purchases, and get cash (U.S. Department of the Treasury 2010a). More than 2.5 million recipients have signed up for the card. By March 2013, all federal benefit payments must be electronic. Recipients have the option of direct deposit into a bank or credit union account or onto the Direct Express® card (U.S. Department of the Treasury 2010a).

Tax refunds are one way of moving forward in advancing electronic government payments. After federal benefits, tax refunds are the single largest source of government paper checks. In 2010, 45 million paper tax refund checks were sent out, costing the government $40 million more than electronic delivery of the refunds (U.S. Department of the Treasury 2010b). These paper checks come with additional costs to the government, but also to consumers if check cashers are used. If the goal is solely saving the government the cost of paper checks, RACs are one option. But RACs come at a high cost to consumers, both in paying for the RAC and in forgoing connections to mainstream financial services.

The *MyAccountCard*—a prepaid card account that can be used to directly deposit tax refunds— meets both government goals of providing tax payments electronically and providing access to the

---

[6] The $1.02 cost of issuing a paper check includes the cost of the paper, envelopes, and postage, as well as back-end costs incurred when checks are lost, forged, stolen, or cannot be delivered (Kuttner 2011).

mainstream financial sector. Tax preparers have their own prepaid card products,[7] but electronic receipt of one's tax refund onto these cards is only available to tax filers using the specific tax preparer. A benefit of offering tax filers a prepaid card account as an integrated part of the tax filing process is that electronic filing (via the prepaid card account) would be available to all tax filers. Also, because of the national scale, the government would be in a position to negotiate a lower cost product and could provide oversight to ensure that the product and its pricing are transparent to consumers.

III. Pilot Overview

The Tax Time Account pilot used a straightforward direct marketing approach, but the design required pilot participants to undertake multiple steps before receiving their tax refund into the prepaid card account. A multistep process would likely not be used in a wider-scale tax-time initiative aimed at facilitating direct deposit and providing accounts to unbanked and underbanked tax filers. An expanded version of the program could, for example, allow filers to indicate directly on their tax forms that they want to receive their refunds via a prepaid card.

The direct marketing approach was used for two key reasons: (1) it was not possible to integrate the prepaid card option into the tax form for the pilot (the tax forms cannot be changed for a subset of the population) and (2) it provides a direct and unbiased test of the different card and marketing features. Direct mail take-up rates for credit cards have been in the 0.3 percent to 0.8 percent range in recent years (Woosley 2007; Kiviat 2010). Data by calendar quarter shows that the take-up rates in the first calendar quarter (the quarter *MyAccountCard* offers were made) tend to be lower and did not exceed 0.5 percent (Kiviat 2010).[8] Although credit cards and prepaid cards are different products, the credit card take-up rates provide a comparison benchmark for the take up rate of card products offered through direct mail. More than 800,000 *MyAccountCard* offers were mailed.

Before the pilot design was finalized, focus groups were conducted in four U.S. cities to obtain low- and moderate-income unbanked and underbanked consumers' reactions to different product features and card pricing, as well as their opinions about product messaging and branding. Focus group findings were used to construct the card features and messages and to develop the *MyAccountCard* brand.

---

[7] Fee schedules differ across prepaid card products, for products offered by tax preparers and those offered outside this market. These cards generally have monthly fees for at least a subset of cardholders (those without a set amount of activity or deposits (e.g., $1,000 per month), ATM fees, and teller fees. A number of prepaid card providers offer cards with a maximum monthly fee below $5 per month, have ATM fees that are $2.50 or less, and offer free bill payment. Other providers offer cards with substantially higher fees. One card, for example, charges a $9.95 monthly fee, $9.95 for electronic bill pay, $19.95 for paper bill pay, and $15.95 to receive a card account closure check.

[8] The direct mail take-up rate for financial products, defined broadly to include credit cards, banking/credit union services, investment services, and insurance products (among others), is 1.01 percent for a prospect list, the type of list used for the pilot (Direct Marketing Association 2010). The take-up rate for credit cards is lower and has been in the 0.3 percent to 0.8 percent range in recent years (Kiviat 2010; Woosley 2007).

The basic steps of the pilot are described below, followed by an overview of the pilot study population, the treatments offered under the pilot, and pilot timing.

- Roughly 800,000 individuals were randomly selected from a population of 8.3 million adults who were likely to be low- and moderate-income (under $35,000 in household income) and were likely to live in an unbanked or underbanked household. The 808,099 people were then randomly assigned into one of eight treatment groups; persons in each treatment group were mailed a letter offering the prepaid card account in early 2011.
- People who received the offer applied for the card account online or by phone and those who satisfied the card-screening requirement were provided with an account number and mailed the prepaid card.[9]
- People filled out their tax returns with their account and routing numbers.
- People received their tax refunds via direct deposit into their card accounts.
- People can use their card accounts for multiple purposes, including ongoing direct deposit of earnings and cash loading, point-of-sale transactions, safe storage of funds, ATM withdrawal, and bill payment.

Putting one's tax refund into the card account was not a requirement of the pilot. People could choose to use their cards continually, without directly depositing their tax refunds into their card accounts. However, the intent of the pilot was to link the tax refund to the card, wherever possible.

The pilot did not include a comprehensive "surround sound" campaign to market the *MyAccountCard* or increase product awareness, because it would introduce opportunities to contaminate comparisons across the different treatment groups. This would happen if the different treatment groups were not equally exposed to the marketing materials. An expanded version of the program could be accompanied by a comprehensive marketing campaign, which would likely increase product take-up.

Pilot Study Population: The Tax Time Account pilot focused on low- and moderate-income people who are likely to be unbanked or underbanked. These adults were identified using commercially available data from Experian Marketing Solutions Inc. To be included in the pilot, the person had to be 19 or older and live in a household that met the following two criteria:

- household was likely to have annual income less than $35,000 and
- household was likely to be unbanked or underbanked.

A valid Social Security number (SSN) was required to sign up for the *MyAccountCard*,[10] so the goal was to limit the pilot sample to people with a SSN. However, this information was not available from Experian Marketing Solutions Inc. As a result, some people who likely received the *MyAccountCard* offer were not eligible. If an expanded version of the program were undertaken, a tax filer individual taxpayer identification number (ITIN) could also be used for card enrollment,

---

[9] Card applications were accepted through April 30, 2011.
[10] This requirement was printed clearly on the offer letter.

which would allow anyone filing a tax return to opt in.[11] For simplicity, the pilot only used the more common SSN.

Experian identified roughly 8.3 million people who met these selection criteria, of whom 808,099 were randomly selected for inclusion in the pilot. Of the letters offering the *MyAccountCard*, an estimated 12.5 percent were not delivered. This rate is higher than the average direct mail return rate of 7.5 percent, although rates can reach 15 percent (UAA Clearinghouse 2010). Letters are generally returned because people move or pass away. Low- and moderate-income people tend to be more transient and move more often than average. We expect that roughly 707,000 card offers were received.[12]

Pilot Treatments: The 808,099 pilot study members were randomly assigned to one of eight treatment groups,[13] with each treatment group including roughly 101,000 adults. All treatment group members were mailed an offer for the *MyAccountCard*. The eight treatment groups differ along three dimensions: (1) no monthly fee versus low monthly fee ($4.95), (2) linked savings account versus no linked savings account, and (3) convenience-focused messaging versus safety-focused messaging.[14] Based on these three categories, the eight treatment groups are as follows:

Group	Monthly Fee	Savings Account	Message
Treatment 1	No fee	Yes	Safety
Treatment 2	No fee	Yes	Convenience
Treatment 3	No fee	No	Safety
Treatment 4	No fee	No	Convenience
Treatment 5	Fee	Yes	Safety
Treatment 6	Fee	Yes	Convenience
Treatment 7	Fee	No	Safety
Treatment 8	Fee	No	Convenience

The pilot evaluation measures the impact of the different offers on the *MyAccountCard* sign-up rate, subsequent card use, and accumulated account balances. For example, people assigned to receive a card with no monthly maintenance fee are compared with those who received a card offer with a monthly maintenance fee to gauge the impact of the fee on take-up and use.[15] Similarly, people who received a card offer without a linked savings account (or safety messaging) are compared with those who are offered a savings account (or convenience messaging). We analyze

---

[11] The ITIN was created by the IRS in the mid-1990s so that foreign nationals and other people not eligible for a SSN can file returns and pay their taxes.

[12] This estimate is based on information received from the Treasury Financial Management Service mail center that received the undelivered letters.

[13] To help ensure comparability across the treatment groups, the sample was drawn using systematic sampling, implicitly stratified by zip code and other characteristics including age, race/ethnicity, gender, and income.

[14] Focus groups conducted prior to the implementation of the pilot (fall 2010) indicated that the Treasury branding was important and added legitimacy to the prepaid card product.

[15] This analysis tests for differences in outcomes across the (randomly assigned) treatment groups. More often, random assignment evaluations test for differences between a single treatment group and a control group, although the two types of analyses follow similarly.

the effect of the different treatments and carry out analyses on the full pilot population and the subgroup of people who accepted the prepaid card offer (i.e., were issued a *MyAccountCard*).

Pilot Timing: On January 18, 2011, 75,000 prepaid card offers were mailed to people in each of the eight treatment groups who live in a subset of states (600,000 offers). About two weeks later, on February 4, 2011, roughly 26,000 additional offers were sent to people in each of the eight treatment groups (about 208,000 offers) who live in the remaining states. This two-tiered mailing was not originally planned but happened consistently across the eight treatment subgroups with exactly the same offer letters.[16] While not a planned feature of the pilot, this two-tiered mailing provides an opportunity to test the effect of the offer letter timing on card take-up and the other outcomes of interest (i.e., we treat the offer letter timing as another treatment).[17]

Pilot Product: The account product used for the pilot was a general purpose reloadable prepaid card that was supplied by Bonneville Bank and its prepaid provider partner Green Dot Corporation. The account was branded MyAccountCard, and was Visa branded. Outside of the changes related to the different treatments it has the following functionality: direct deposit, cash loading, ATM withdrawal and balance inquiry (in network and out of network), online bill payment, point-of-sale purchasing wherever Visa is accepted, cash back at point of sale, Visa's Zero Liability policy, FDIC pass-through insurance, and no overdraft capability. Pricing for all services on the card are in the table below.

Service	Fee
Monthly service	Depending on offer either: $4.95 (Waived in any month when loaded at least $1,000 into account or have 30 posted purchases) Or $0
Card acquisition	Free
ATM cash withdrawals at in-network	Free (15,000 locations nationwide)
Transactions at U.S. merchant locations, online or over the phone	Free
Cash back with purchases	Free
Online bill pay	Free
Balance inquiries online, by phone, in-network ATMs, and by text (standard text messaging rates may apply from the wireless carrier)	Free
Add money to the card account with direct deposit	Free
Lost/stolen card replacement or second card	$4.95

---

[16] A data-sorting error in the final stages of sample selection resulted in the first round of 600,000 letters being sent to a subset of states (based on zip code), instead of all states as planned. Letters were not sent to some Midwestern states and all Western states. To address the error, roughly 26,000 additional offers were sent to people in each of the eight treatment groups who live in states excluded in the first mailing.

[17] Since the two mailings targeted different states, these analyses, strictly speaking, provide a joint test of (1) receiving the offer letter in February (versus January) and (2) living in the states that received the second mailing (versus the first mailing). Since we have no reason to believe there is strong geographic variation, we interpret the finding as providing information about the offer timing.

Out-of-network ATM cash withdrawals	$2.50 plus any fee the ATM owner charges
Teller cash withdrawals	$2.50
Balance inquiries at out-of-network ATMs	$0.50
Add money in-person at participating retail locations	Up to $0.95
Card use outside of the 50 United States	3% of transaction amount

IV. Data and Measures

The analysis combines prepaid card data from Bonneville/Green Dot, demographic data from Experian, and zip code-level IRS data. The final sample size includes all 808,099 pilot participants.[18]

Prepaid Card Data: The primary data for the evaluation are anonymous[19] individual-level data from Bonneville/Green Dot, the *MyAccountCard* provider. These data provide information on pilot participants, including card enrollment, tax refund receipt (federal and state) into the card account, card-use activity, accumulated balances, and fees. Card activity is tracked and provided monthly and the analysis includes data from January 2011 (the first month card offers were sent) through the end of July 2011 (the last month of data used in the analysis). With this timeframe and the timing of card take-up, most *MyAccountCard* cardholders (i.e., those issued a prepaid card) had their cards about half a year (between 5.5 and 6.5 months).[20]

Measures of card activity capture any use over the period (e.g., had ever used direct deposit), as well as ongoing card use. To learn about ongoing card use, use is examined over time as well as in the last month—for example, average account balances over the pilot (from card issuance through July 2011) and account balance in July 2011. Activity in the last month examined is an indication of ongoing use, because 80 percent of people who used their cards in last month (July 2011) also used their cards in the prior month. Key measures examined in the analyses, along with a description of the variable, are presented in table 1. These variables are grouped into six categories: card application and issuance, card use (e.g., card activation and subsequent duration of use), direct deposit into card account (i.e., tax refunds and other direct deposit), card account balances, card account fees, and card account management.

Demographic Characteristics: The prepaid card data from Green Dot/Bonneville are augmented with individual- and household-level demographic and economic data obtained from Experian Marketing Solutions Inc. The individual-level characteristics include age, race/ethnicity, and gender, and the household-level variables include presence of children, income range (<$15,000, $15,000–$24,999, and $25,000–$34,999), and a measure of the household's likelihood of being unbanked or underbanked (described below). We expect card take-up and use to be greater among younger households with children because they are more likely to receive a tax refund as a

---

[18] Multiple imputation is used to impute missing values in the Experian and IRS data.

[19] The individual-level data do not include personally identifying information (e.g., name, address, date of birth, or SSN).

[20] Seventy percent of cardholders were issued their cards by January 31, 2011, and over 90 percent of cardholders were issued their cards before February 15, 2011.

result of the EITC.[21] Similarly, we expect older adults to take up and use the card at lower rates, since many retired households do not have to file federal income taxes. Lower-income households and those with a greater likelihood of being unbanked or underbanked are expected to have a greater need for a low-cost transaction account, so are hypothesized to take up and use the card to a greater extent.

The individual- and household-level characteristics are constructed by Experian using information from multiple sources. Exact information is available in some cases, but values are estimated in other cases. Date of birth, for example, is acquired from public and proprietary files with exact date of birth available for roughly 70 percent of persons; age is estimated for the remaining 30 percent. Other variables, such as household income and the likelihood of being unbanked or underbanked, are fully predicted based on individual-, household-, and zip code–level variables. For household income, statistical models are used to predict and assign households to one of 12 income ranges. Our analysis focuses on households in the bottom three income ranges (shown above). The household likelihood of being unbanked or underbanked is based on a statistical model that produces an underbanked score, where values between 1 and 9 identify households likely to be unbanked or underbanked. A value of 1 indicates the households most likely to be unbanked/underbanked and successively higher values indicate a lower likelihood of being unbanked/underbanked.[22]

Pilot participants are on average 46 years old and evenly split between white and nonwhite (table 2, column 1). All participants have annual incomes below $35,000, with roughly a third in each of the three income categories (<$15,000, $15,000–$24,999, and $25,000–$34,999). The average underbanked score of 5 falls in the middle of the 1–9 range, and the percentage of pilot participants in the lower (score 1–3), middle (score 4–6), and upper (score 7–9) ranges are 34 percent, 28 percent, and 38 percent, respectively.

Zip code–level characteristics: The analysis also includes zip code–level characteristics about where pilot participants live. Information designed to get at ease of use and potential costs and benefits of use includes the number of card-reload locations and the number of free ATMs in the zip code. The analysis also incorporates zip code–level IRS tax return information from tax-filing season 2010.[23] The specific variables are the percentage of returns receiving the earned income tax

---

[21] The available data indicate that 15 percent of pilot participants live in households with at least one child. For the remaining 85 percent of pilot participants, we do not know whether children are in the household. For this reason, the estimated relationship between presence of children in the household and the outcomes of interest are lower-bound estimates.

[22] Since all Experian demographic and economic variables are at least partially predicted, they are measured with some error. For example, as part of their income validation process, Experian compares results from their income model with reports from a survey (for a sample of households). The results suggest that their accuracy rate for households with incomes below $15,000 is 85 percent, while their accuracy rate for incomes below $35,000 is about 70 percent. Because the Experian characteristics are imprecise, we estimate models that both include and exclude these characteristics. The results are not sensitive to the model specification. The primary specification includes the Experian variables because they provide insight into how demographic and economic characteristics relate to card take-up and use.

[23] If the Treasury pilot affected whether and the way people filed their federal taxes in 2011 (e.g., paid versus self-prepared), then including 2011 IRS tax return data in the analysis could lead to biased estimates. For this reason, the

credit (EITC), receiving a deduction for student loan interest, being filed by a third party (paid or volunteer versus self), and being filed with an ITIN versus a SSN.

Zip codes with high rates of EITC receipt have many low- and moderate-income families with children. In these areas, tax filers may receive large tax refunds and may not have bank accounts, so may be more likely to benefit from, and thus take up and use, a prepaid card offered at tax time. Similarly, zip codes with a high fraction of tax filers who receive a deduction for student loan interest may identify areas where young people are just starting off and could benefit from the prepaid card product. Greater use of paid or voluntary preparers could signal areas where people need help preparing their income tax returns, possibly as the result of claiming the EITC and other tax credits. Finally, pilot participants in zip codes with a high fraction of tax returns filed with an ITIN (versus a SSN) may themselves not have a SSN, so be ineligible to receive the *MyAccountCard*. Thus, we expect lower take-up and use of the *MyAccountCard* among people living in these zip codes. The analysis also incorporates information on whether the zip code is rural, suburban, or urban. Individuals in rural and suburban areas (relative to those in urban areas) may have more limited access to financial institutions, so have a greater need for a prepaid card product.

V. Analytic Approach
Verifying Random Assignment
To evaluate the random assignment into the eight treatment groups, we examine characteristics of the pilot sample by treatment group. If the random assignment occurred without systematic bias, then people in the different treatment groups should look similar across the measured characteristic. For each baseline characteristic, we test whether there are any statistically significant differences in mean characteristics across people assigned to the treatment groups with (1) a monthly maintenance fee versus no monthly maintenance fee, (2) a linked savings account versus no linked savings account, and (3) convenience-focused messaging versus safety-focused messaging.

Randomization into the eight treatment groups was stratified by the individual- and household-level characteristics available in the Experian file (age, race/ethnicity, gender, presence of children, income, and underbanked score), so the treatment groups should look similar along these dimensions. In fact, there are no statistically significant differences in the individual- and household-level characteristics across the treatment groups (table 2, columns 2–7). Randomization was not stratified by the zip code–level characteristics, and there are some statistically significant differences in the zip code–level characteristics across treatment groups. However, the values across treatment groups are qualitatively identical. For example, statistically speaking, the average number of *MyAccountCard* reload locations per zip code differs for persons in the linked savings account versus no linked savings account groups, but the numbers are nearly identical (4.69 versus 4.67,

---

analysis includes IRS data from tax-filing season 2010 (prior to the Treasury pilot). An analysis of 2010 and 2011 tax return data shows they are highly correlated across these two years; the correlation coefficients are between 0.96 and 0.99.

respectively). Based on the available data, we conclude that randomization across the treatment groups was successful.

Empirical Model

Analyses are carried out on the full pilot sample, as well as on the subpopulation of people who were issued the *MyAccountCard* (i.e., cardholders). All these analyses compare treatment groups, such as those with and without a monthly fee and those with and without a linked savings account. Descriptions of the analyses for each of the two samples are provided, in turn, below.

Analyses of Full Pilot Sample: These analyses estimate the causal impact of the different card offers on a series of outcomes including card take-up, receipt of tax refund into the card account, card account balances, and account fees (see table 1). The basic method for estimating the causal impact would compare mean outcomes for each group. Although the analysis of baseline characteristics shows qualitatively identical characteristics for those offered the different treatments, we use a regression-based method to control for measured individual-, household-, and zip code–level characteristics.[24] Including these variables in the model also provides information on how these characteristics relate to card take-up and use. Separate models are estimated for each outcome.

The specific form of the model depends on the outcome being analyzed. For binary outcomes, such as whether a person applies for the card (yes=1/no=0), we estimate probit models. Probit models are designed to deal with the dichotomous nature of the dependent variables. For outcomes that are continuous in nature, such as card balances, we use linear models. The model for each outcome includes a series of explanatory variables and key among them are indicators of the treatment group: (1) monthly fee versus no monthly fee, (2) linked savings account versus no linked savings account, and (3) safety messaging versus convenience messaging. Beyond the treatment variables, the model includes an indicator of whether the pilot participant was in the February 4, 2011 (versus January 18, 2011) mailing group. Since low- and moderate-income tax filers tend to file their taxes in late January or early February, we expect fewer in the second mail group to take up the *MyAccountCard*, and this is confirmed in the results. Each regression model also includes individual- and household-level characteristics (e.g., age, race/ethnicity, and income) and zip code–level characteristics (e.g., number of free ATMs and percentage of tax returns receiving the EITC). Details of the model specification are presented in appendix A.

The analysis also tests for interaction effects in the treatment groups. This allows us to test whether there are any impacts from particular combinations of treatments. For example, we can determine whether the linked savings account feature is more effective when combined with no monthly fee versus a monthly fee. Overall, the analyses show no interactions between the treatments.[25]

---

[24] Including these measures helps account for the residual variation in the outcome measures, thereby providing more precise impact estimates.

[25] We test for interaction effects (between each of the three treatment groups) for each outcome and only one interaction is statistically significantly different from zero (at the 5 percent level)—the interaction between the linked savings

Analyses of Cardholder: In addition to examining the outcomes for the full pilot population, we examine outcomes for the subpopulation of people who were issued the *MyAccountCard*. *MyAccountCard* cardholders are not a random subset of each treatment group, so these analyses do not provide impact (i.e., causal) estimates. Rather, they provide more descriptive information on the relationship between card features and card use (e.g., account balances and account fees).

To get a sense of whether the characteristics of cardholders in the different treatment groups differ, we test whether there are any statistically significant differences in the cardholder characteristics across the groups. We find that cardholders in the monthly fee/no monthly fee treatment groups differ along three dimensions (gender, underbanked score, and percentage of tax returns receiving the EITC), while the cardholders in the linked savings/no linked savings and safety/convenience messaging treatment groups do not differ significantly along any of the dimensions tested (table 3). While there are few differences in observed characteristics across cardholder groups, there could be differences in unobserved characteristics. Thus, as mentioned above, results from the cardholder analyses cannot be interpreted as causal, because estimated differences between cardholder groups could be due (in part or whole) to differences in cardholder characteristics.

Analyses focused on *MyAccountCard* cardholders are nonetheless important, because they provide information beyond what can be gleaned from analyses of the full pilot sample. Analyses of card use for the full pilot sample (i.e., cardholders and non-cardholders combined) confound card take-up with card use. For example, while we expect people with no monthly maintenance fee to incur lower fees on average than people who face a $4.95 monthly maintenance fee, we find that people who received the no monthly maintenance fee card offer have significantly higher total fees. This result is generated because substantially more individuals who received the no monthly maintenance fee offer took up and are using the *MyAccountCard*. Looking at findings based on both the full pilot population and the subpopulation of *MyAccountCard* cardholders provides a broader understanding of the pilot program and the relative influence of the different card features.

VI. Pilot Results

This section provides the pilot findings structured around four research questions:

1. Who applied for and used the *MyAccountCard*?
2. How do cardholders use the *MyAccountCard*?
3. How do *MyAccountCard* features and card messaging influence card take-up and use?
4. How do individual- and local-level characteristics influence use of the *MyAccountCard*?

The first two research questions are addressed descriptively (table 4), while the last two questions are answered using the regression models described above (table 5).

---

account and safety messaging treatment groups in the average variable fee model. Given the large number of models and outcomes tested, we expect at least one of these coefficients to be statistically significant based on chance.

Who Applied for and Received the MyAccountCard?

Overall, 1,967 people (0.3 percent) who received a *MyAccountCard* offer applied for the card, of which 1,933 people (98.3 percent) were issued a *MyAccountCard* (table 4). This 0.3 percent take-up is in the 0.3 to 0.5 range of take-up rates for credit cards in the first calendar quarter, although at the lower end of the range. Some elements of the pilot could have lowered the take-up rate. Top among them are (1) the quality of the Experian mailing list (addresses and characteristics) and (2) the timing of the offer letters. First, roughly 100,000 of the mailed letters were not delivered and it is unclear if all of the remaining letters were received by the intended recipient.[26] Also, only people with a SSN were eligible for the *MyAccountCard*, but it was not possible to restrict the mailing list to this subpopulation, as these data were not available. Thus, the offer was likely mailed to people not eligible for the card. Other important targeting variables such as household income and the likelihood of being unbanked/underbanked are based on model predictions, so some offers possibly went to higher-income people firmly in the financial mainstream with less need for a card account. Second, even the earlier mailing of January 18, 2011 (versus February 4, 2011), may not have been ideal. Because low- and moderate-income tax filers tend to file their taxes early in the season (starting in late January), interest in the *MyAccountCard* may have been higher if people had received their offer letters in early January.[27] Other elements that could have lowered take-up are absence of a surround sound campaign, a multistep process for receiving one's tax refund into the card account, and unfamiliarity with the government offering such a product (people could have thought it was scam). While some of these items were apparent at the start of the pilot, they were accepted as part of its design since the pilot was constructed around evaluating card design features and messaging approaches, not overall take-up in a national campaign.

Take-up of the *MyAccountCard* varies across subsets of the pilot population. The highest take-up rate is among those most likely to be unbanked (those with the lowest underbanked score). These individuals had a take-up rate of 0.8 percent—nearly three times higher than the take-up rate for the full pilot population (not shown). Females, households with children, and households with incomes below $15,000 were also more likely to take up the card, although not nearly to the same extent. Females and people living in households with children were 45 percent and 35 percent (respectively) more likely to take up the *MyAccountCard* than were males and people living in households without children, while people in households with incomes below $15,000 were 17 percent more likely to take up the card than those with higher incomes. All these differences are statistically significant at the 1 percent level.

The timing of the card offer is important for take-up. The findings clearly indicate that earlier is better. People who were mailed the offer in mid-January were 85 percent more likely to apply for the card than those who were mailed the offer in early February. It therefore seems likely that mailing the offer in late December or early January would have resulted in higher take-up. In

---

[26] The 0.3 percent take-up rate accounts for the roughly 100,000 letters that were not delivered (see table 4).

[27] Under the original pilot design, the mailing schedule was such that the offer letters were to arrive in people's mailboxes early in the week of January 4, 2011. Federal notification requirements for a Systems of Records Notice delayed the mailing by roughly three weeks.

moving forward with any potential future options for using tax refunds as a way to deliver mainstream financial products, information about the prepaid card program should be distributed before the tax-filing season begins.

How Do Cardholders Use the MyAccountCard?

Of the 1,933 people who were issued a *MyAccountCard* (i.e., cardholders), 33 percent used their card within the first six months of the program (table 4). It is not clear why two-thirds of people issued the *MyAccountCard* never used it. Part of the explanation could lie in the multistep process for receiving one's tax refund into the card account. Some people may have found the multiple steps too cumbersome or possibly forgot to bring their cards (or account number) to their tax preparation sessions, and then chose not to subsequently activate the cards. Among the subpopulation of cardholders who used their cards in the first six months of the pilot (i.e., active cardholders), nearly half (46 percent) used their cards half the months they had them. Over a third (37 percent) were still using their cards in the last month examined (July 2011).

Only a subset of cardholders directly deposited their tax refunds into the card accounts. Sixteen percent of all cardholders and 48 percent of active cardholders did so. Over half of these deposits were made in February and over 80 percent were made by the end of March. The timing of the card offers (mid-January and early February) could have influenced this use of the card. Also, since the *MyAccountCard* cannot be used to pay for tax preparation, cardholders without the resources to cover these costs may have turned to a RAC.[28] Other types of direct deposits (e.g., earnings from an employer or government benefits) were used by a total of 15 percent of cardholders, with 5 percent using direct deposit in the last month examined. Among cardholders who ever used the direct deposit feature, 46 percent made one deposit, 13 percent made two deposits, and 41 percent made three or more deposits (not shown).

In general, the *MyAccountCard* balances are modest and few cardholders built up their account balances over time. Card balances are calculated using the lowest transaction account balance in a month (to get a sense of the reserve funds cardholders accumulate) combined with the end of month savings account balance.[29] Among active cardholders, the average account balance over the first six months was $52, although the average balance in July was roughly half that ($25). The average decline in account balances results, in part, from people depositing their tax refunds into the card accounts and then drawing down the funds.

Fees are relatively common among cardholders, although the fees for people actively using their cards fell across the pilot period. Seventy-six percent of active cardholders incurred at least one variable fee (i.e., non-monthly maintenance fee). The most common was ATM withdrawal fees. Seventy-four percent of active cardholders had an ATM withdrawal fee, while 14 percent incurred

---

[28] As mentioned above, research finds that nearly half of RAL and RAC users cite paying for tax preparation as an important reason for taking out the RAL or RAC (Barr and Dokko 2008).

[29] Using the end of month savings account balance allows transfer from the transaction account to the savings account to be accurately captured. Savings account balances do not have a large influence on overall account balances, as only 1.4 percent of cardholders offered a savings account deposited money into a savings account in the first six months of the pilot (discussed below).

another variable fee.[30] The average monthly variable fee among active cardholders across the first six months of the pilot was $5.11, but was $3.16 among cardholders who used their cards in July. Among cardholders subject to a monthly maintenance fee, 17 percent avoided the monthly fee during at least one month by reaching deposits of $1,000 or having 30 transaction purchases. Of these cardholders, 69 percent avoided the fee during one month, 16 percent during two months, and 15 percent during three or more months. Under this pilot program, the monthly maintenance fee cannot take a customer's balance below $0, so some cardholders avoided it (or paid less than $4.95) because they had a zero balance (i.e., did not have the full $4.95 in their accounts). In the last month examined (July 2011), people who used their *MyAccountCard* paid an average of $3.89 in total fees, $3.16 in variable fees, and $3.01 in ATM fees.

The online account management features were not used by many cardholders. Among active cardholders, less than half (43 percent) ever logged into their accounts online, although 54 percent set up online account management. Fewer active cardholders—roughly 36 percent—activated the *MyAccountCard* text messaging feature. Only 12 percent of active cardholders either sent or received a text message related to their account.

By and large, the linked savings accounts were not well utilized. Among cardholders offered a linked savings account, 12.6 percent opened an account and only 1.4 percent deposited money into the account within the first six months of the program (not shown). The process for setting up the savings account may help explain the limited use of these accounts. While participants could sign up for the *MyAccountCard* by phone or online, the savings account could not be activated over the phone; it required a second step to set up the account online. Only 1.2 percent of cardholders who were eligible for the linked savings account and signed up for the *MyAccountCard* by phone activated the linked savings account. The comparable percentage for people who signed up for the *MyAccountCard* online is 35.7 percent. This finding is consistent with research from behavioral economics that shows people are more likely to undertake a particular action if the process for doing so is made easy.

Another drawback of the linked savings account is that deposits can only be made via transfers from the transaction account to the savings account. One cannot, for example, directly deposit a portion of earnings or the tax refund directly into the savings account; the funds must be deposited into the transaction account and then be transferred to the savings account. The two-step process creates an additional hurdle and may reduce use of the savings account for low- and moderate-income consumers.

How Do MyAccountCard Features and Card Messaging Influence Card Take-Up and Use?

Only one of the tested features—card cost—stands out as influencing the behavior of pilot participants in a significant and consistent way. Charging a $4.95 monthly maintenance fee (versus no monthly maintenance fee) for the *MyAccountCard* reduced card applications, issuance, and transactional use by 40 to 55 percent. The linked savings account feature did not significantly

---

[30] See table 1 for list of variable fees.

increase card applications or use, nor is there evidence that it led to greater savings. Similarly, product messaging (safety versus convenience) did not significantly influence pilot participant behavior. Detailed pilot findings by card feature—card cost, linked savings account, messaging— are described in turn below.

Cost of the MyAccountCard

Charging a $4.95 monthly maintenance fee (versus no monthly maintenance fee) decreased *MyAccountCard* applications and issuance by 42 and 43 percent, respectively (table 5, column 1).[31,][32] The estimated own-price elasticity of demand implies that a 10 percent increase in the monthly cost of the *MyAccountCard* reduces card applications and issuance by 2.6 percent.[33] Similarly, a 100 percent increase in the monthly cost of the card, say from $2 to $4, is expected to reduce card applications and issuance by 26 percent.[34] A study by Barr, Dokko, and Feit (2011), based on a survey of low- and moderate-income households in Detroit, also finds that consumers are sensitive to monthly card fees, although the magnitudes are smaller than the impact estimates found here. They find that card take-up rates fall by 28 percent when the monthly fee increases from $0 to $9.95 (Barr et al. 2011, p. 20).

In addition to examining the full population, we also examine whether different subpopulations are more or less price sensitive. We find that women and people in households likely to be unbanked are somewhat less price sensitive, although the results are only marginally statistically significant (at the 10 percent level). Unbanked households may be more likely to pay a monthly fee for the prepaid cards because they have fewer options.

Card use also decreases with the presence of the $4.95 monthly maintenance fee. The likelihood of using the card within the first six months of the pilot was 47 percent lower for people offered a card with the monthly fee. In this case, the estimated own-price elasticity of demand implies that a 10 percent increase in the monthly cost of the *MyAccountCard* reduces card use by 2.9 percent. Longer-term measures of card use are also lower among pilot participants who face the monthly fee. People offered a card with the $4.95 monthly fee (versus no monthly fee) used the card

---

[31] A complete set of estimated probit coefficients from selected regression equations is presented in appendix table A-1.

[32] The percentage change in the outcome variable (e.g., card application) that coincides with a movement from no monthly fee to a $4.95 monthly fee is calculated as "the difference in the predicted probability of card take-up with and without the monthly fee" divided by "the predicted probability of card take-up without the monthly fee." The predicted probabilities are based on individuals' own characteristics, rather than on the average characteristics of the pilot sample. More specifically, the predicted probability of card take-up without the monthly fee is calculated for each person using their own characteristics but assuming each person has no monthly fee; and then averaging the probabilities over the pilot sample.

[33] We calculate the estimated own-price elasticity of demand using the arc (i.e., midpoint) elasticity of demand formula. With only two data points (no monthly fee and $4.95 monthly fee), the estimated elasticity assumes that the percentage decline in card take-up that results from a specified percent increase in the monthly fee is the same across the $0 to $4.95 range. While there is likely variation over this range, the calculation of an elasticity provides a reasonable basis for considering different price points along the $0 to $4.95 continuum.

[34] That a higher price leads to lower demand for the product is not surprising and is consistent with economic theory (i.e., the demand curve for a product is downward sloping). The magnitude of the effect is the key element, as it provides information on the degree to which people are price sensitive with respect to prepaid card costs.

50 percent fewer months and were 55 percent less likely to use the card in the last month examined (July 2011).

Analyses based on the subset of people *issued* a *MyAccountCard* suggest that the lower use of the *MyAccountCard* among the monthly fee group is driven (at least in part) by their lower take-up of the card. Analyses of the cardholder sample find that card use is significantly lower among cardholders in the monthly fee group (versus in the no monthly fee group) for only one of the four card-use outcomes (table 5, column 2). Specifically, cardholders in the monthly fee treatment group used the *MyAccountCard* 15 percent fewer months than people in the no monthly fee group. This finding suggests that the ongoing nature of the monthly fee (as long as there are funds in the card account) may lead some cardholders to stop using the card. However, as mentioned above, the other three card-use measures do not show statistically significant differences in card use among the two monthly fee groups. These results show that cardholders who are not charged a monthly fee value the card and continue to use it (i.e., they value the card even though the monthly fee is zero).[35]

An analysis of tax refunds and other direct deposits to the *MyAccountCard* shows a similar pattern. People offered a card with the $4.95 monthly maintenance fee (versus no monthly maintenance fee) were 52 percent less likely to directly deposit a tax refund into their card accounts and 38 percent less likely to make other types of direct deposits. But, among the subset of *MyAccountCard* cardholders, there are no statistically significant differences in the use of direct deposit between the two groups. Consistent with the discussion above, these results show that the presence of the $4.95 monthly fee influences card take-up, but that the behavior of cardholders is similar among those who do and do not have to pay the monthly fee.

Card account balances are lower among people with (versus without) the monthly fee. This pattern exists among all pilot participants and among the subgroup of *MyAccountCard* cardholders. Among *MyAccountCard* cardholders, for example, the average account balance during the first six months of the pilot was $14.90 lower for people who face a $4.95 monthly fee. Similarly, the account balance in the last month examined (July 2011) was an average of $12.27 lower for those with a monthly fee. The lower card balances among people with a $4.95 monthly maintenance fee are likely linked to the monthly maintenance fee. Since most pilot participants were not issued a *MyAccountCard*, the difference in account balance values for the full pilot population is small, although statistically significantly different from zero.

Among all pilot participants, those in the monthly fee (versus no monthly fee) group paid less in average variable fees over the first six months. While this difference is statistically significant, its magnitude is less than one cent when looking across all pilot participants. The three measures of card account fees that capture fees paid in the last month examined (July 2011) show no statistically significant differences between the two treatment groups. Among *MyAccountCard* cardholders, the pattern is slightly different. Cardholders in the monthly fee treatment group incurred higher *total* account fees in July 2011 (by $0.28 on average), but did not pay more in variable fees or ATM fees

---

[35] One could imagine a scenario in which people offered the free card take it up because it has a zero fixed cost, but place little value on the card.

in July. At first glance, one might expect the difference in total fees to be larger than $0.28 between these two groups. However, the monthly maintenance fee is less than $4.95 for many cardholders in the monthly fee treatment group, which happens if the cardholder deposits $1,000 in a month, has 30 transaction purchases in a month, or does not have funds to cover the monthly fee.

Among *MyAccountCard* cardholders, people with a $4.95 monthly fee (versus no monthly fee) were significantly less likely to have logged into their online account and to have used text messaging. There is no clear reason why use of these account management features should differ across these two groups.

Overall, these results suggest that people are sensitive to the cost of the *MyAccountCard*. People who face the $4.95 monthly maintenance fee were less likely to take up and use the *MyAccountCard*. Among persons who became cardholders, there is some evidence that people in the monthly fee treatment group used the card less over time and had lower account balances.

Linked Savings Account
Outcomes for pilot participants offered and not offered the linked savings account show few differences. Adults offered the linked savings account (versus not offered the linked savings account) were not significantly more likely to apply for or be issued a *MyAccountCard* (table 5, column 3).

One consistent difference between pilot participants who were and were not offered a linked savings account is that those offered the linked savings account used the card less. The significantly lower rates of card use appear for the longer-term measures of use. People offered a card with the linked savings account were 24 percent less likely to use the card in half of the months and 28 percent less likely to use the card in the last month examined, July 2011 (table 5, column 4). We see a similar pattern among the subsample of cardholders. In this case, the percentages are 27 percent and 30 percent, respectively. It is not clear how the presence of a linked savings account would lead individuals to use the card differently over time. However, it is possible that people's expectations about what they could achieve with the card differed across the two groups and that people with the linked savings account who were not able to save or reach a savings goal became discouraged.

The availability of a linked savings account did not significantly influence any of the other outcomes examined—direct deposit of tax refunds, other types of direct deposits, card account balances, card account fees, or card account management.

It costs roughly $1 per month to provide a prepaid card customer with a linked savings account. Findings from this pilot suggest that these resources would be better used by reducing the monthly cost of the prepaid card. This is not to say that linked savings accounts are not a useful tool, but rather that targeting the linked savings accounts to people who can most benefit from them would be more cost effective (versus providing them to everyone). For example, cardholders who successfully maintain a minimum account balance (of say $50) for three months could be made eligible for the linked savings account.

Product Messaging—Safety versus Convenience

The type of product messaging—safety versus convenience—did not significantly influence card take-up or use (table 5, columns 5 and 6). Of all the outcomes examined, the only difference between the two groups is that cardholders who received the safety messaging were 26 percent more likely to set up and use an online account. Both the safety-focused and convenience-focused messaging mentioned the online account (and text messaging) was available, and nothing specific in the safety-focused messaging appears to account for this difference. Any future version of this program would likely benefit from highlighting that the card account can offer a fast, convenient, and safe way to receive one's federal tax refund.

How Do Individual- and Local-Level Characteristics Influence Use of the MyAccountCard?

By and large, results from the regression models that control for the individual-, household-, and zip code-level characteristics show that the individual and household characteristics affect card take-up and use in the expected directions. Individuals in households with low unbanked scores (i.e., likely to be unbanked) are more likely to apply for and be issued a *MyAccountCard*, use the card more consistently over the first six months of the pilot, and have a tax refund directly deposited into the *MyAccountCard*. For example, as compared with pilot participants least likely to be unbanked (score of 9), participants most likely to be unbanked (score of 1) are (1) 3.1 times more likely to apply for and be issued a card, (2) 2.6 times more likely to use the card half of the months they have it, and (3) 2.4 times more likely to deposit their tax refunds directly into their card accounts. These findings highlight the greater need for and use of the account among people most likely to be unbanked. Household income is not significantly related to any of the outcomes examined, although the pilot sample is restricted to persons with household incomes below $35,000.

Age, gender, presence of children in the household, and race/ethnicity are also significant predictors of card take-up and use. People ages 65 and older are the least likely to take up and use the card, which may reflect their lesser need for a transactional product and lower likelihood of filing a tax return. Females and households with children are more likely to apply for, be issued, and use the *MyAccountCard*. For example, as compared with males, females are 28 percent more likely to apply for the card, 59 percent more likely to use the card half of the months, and 67 percent more likely to directly deposit their tax refunds into the card account. African Americans applied for and were issued the *MyAccountCard* at higher rates than whites, while Hispanics and Asians were less likely to do so.

The number of card reload locations and free ATMs in one's zip code is not significantly related to card application, issuance, or card use. The urbanicity of one's zip code is generally not related to card take-up or use, with one exception. People in rural areas were 38 percent more likely to directly deposit their tax refunds into their *MyAccountCard* than people in urban areas. Beyond this, we find that people living in zip codes with a high fraction of tax filers who receive the EITC, use a paid preparer, and receive a student loan tax deduction were more likely to apply for and be issued the *MyAccountCard*, but were not more likely to directly deposit their tax refunds into the card account.

VII. Discussion of Findings

The results of the Tax Time Account direct mail pilot offer a number of lessons that will be helpful when evaluating future options that could, for example, integrate an account option into the tax-filing and refund process.

In terms of effectiveness, at the most basic level, the pilot established proof of concept for offering a card account in conjunction with tax time. Offering and issuing cards in this way, and delivering tax refunds to those card accounts, proved feasible for Treasury at an operational level. In the course of the pilot itself, nearly 2,000 cards were issued, and roughly half of active cardholders, or approximately 300 users, received tax refunds into their card accounts.

In addition, the pilot established that there is a market and demand for such a product. Take-up rates were in line with expectations for a direct mail offer of a financial product. Moreover, take-up rates varied across groups in a manner consistent with the product serving a need for unbanked and underbanked populations. Most noticeably, individuals in the pilot sample with the highest propensity to be unbanked were three times more likely to apply for the card and nearly 2.5 times more likely to use the card to receive a tax refund as those in the sample with the lowest propensity to be unbanked. That direct mail take-up rates are, in absolute terms, low, serves primarily to underscore the importance of Treasury streamlining the delivery process at scale, such as by offering the card directly in the tax-filing and refund process.

A final and central set of lessons for card effectiveness concerns the impacts of product features on the take-up and use of such a card. The pilot established evidence on the degree of price sensitivity in card take-up: a $4.95 monthly fee cut take-up nearly in half, relative to a card with no monthly fee. The other card feature tested, the availability of a savings account, did not have significant effects on take-up, and, if anything, was associated with diminished use. The savings account features tested in the pilot were less than ideal, as savings account activation required additional cardholder action (i.e., online activation) and deposits could not be made directly into the savings account (i.e., only transfers from the transaction account are allowed); it is possible that different implementation of a savings account feature would have produced different results. Nonetheless, the implications of the pilot results for a national rollout suggest that Treasury direct its efforts primarily toward securing the availability of a low monthly fee card, even at the expense of additional card features. The pilot suggests that for every $0.50 Treasury can reduce the monthly fee below $4.95, an additional 2.6 percent of eligible individuals may take up the card.

In terms of efficiency, the results from the pilot, offer limited insight into the net benefit from future efforts that could be integrated into the tax-filing and refund process. The main financial benefit to Treasury from the account is known and comes in cost savings associated with delivering tax refunds electronically: it costs 10 cents to process electronic refunds versus $1.02 for paper. The primary costs to Treasury from an effort integrated into the tax filing and refund process would be significantly different than the pilot. Further work would be needed to estimate the costs of such efforts. Operational details would need to be finalized before a cost estimate could be developed.

VIII. Conclusion

The federal government's creating an option for low- and moderate-income tax filers to receive refunds directly onto a low-cost, account-linked card, as tested in this pilot, is a concept with promise. Such a card can reduce costs to Treasury by reducing the number of costly paper checks used to deliver refunds. And such considerations are only one dimension of the potential benefits such a card could offer. Individuals who take up such a card presumably derive private benefits from card ownership and use. Such a product might also reduce the need for and use of high-cost tax return options such as RACs, especially if it can be used to pay for tax preparation. And for those without a bank account, such a product could bring benefits of access to mainstream financial services.

This pilot produced a set of valuable lessons for how best to realize that promise in future efforts. Tests focusing on the card's design features suggest that individuals are price sensitive with respect to monthly fees, and that linked savings accounts (at least as designed in this pilot) were not perceived as valuable. Tests for the impact of messaging emphasis, focusing on either safety or convenience, found no difference in response.

Overall, pilot results suggest that such a product could be both valuable to tax filers and cost saving to Treasury. Pilot results generally indicate that, if it were determined to expand beyond a pilot, Treasury should focus on customer needs in at least two ways: First, efforts should be made to make available as low cost a card as is possible without subsidy. Second, the process for acquiring the card and using it to receive a tax refund should be as streamlined as possible, such as including the card as an option directly on the tax form itself.

Finally, additional operational challenges not tested as part of this pilot merit further attention in developing such a product for national rollout. A key limitation in this pilot was that adoption of the card required individuals to pay for tax preparation out of pocket (in contrast with, for example, RACs). Since many low- and moderate-income tax filers do not have the means to pay for tax preparation services upfront, future investigations should consider the feasibility of allowing payment of tax preparation fees out of the tax refund as part of adoption of the card.

IX. References

Barr, Michael, and Jane Dokko. 2008. "Third-Party Tax Administration: The Case of Low- and Moderate-Income Households." *Journal of Empirical Legal Studies* 5(4).

Barr, Michael, Jane Dokko, and Eleanor Feit. 2011. "Preferences for Banking and Payment Services among Low- and Moderate-Income Households." *Finance and Economics Discussion Series Working Paper 2011-13*. Washington, DC: Federal Reserve Board.

Board of Governors of the Federal Reserve System. 2011. "Report to the Congress on Government-Administered, General-Use Prepaid Cards." Washington, DC: Federal Reserve System.

Chakravorti, Sujit, and Victor Lubasi. 2006. "Payment Instrument Choice: The Case of Prepaid Cards." *Economic Perspectives* 2. Chicago, IL: Federal Reserve Bank of Chicago.

Direct Marketing Association. 2010. "The 2010 Response Rate Report: Performance and Cost Metrics across Direct Media." New York: Direct Marketing Association.

Elliehausen, Gregory. 2005. "Consumer Use of Tax Refund Anticipation Loans." Credit Research Center Monograph 37. Washington, DC: Georgetown University.

Federal Deposit Insurance Corporation (FDIC). 2009. "National Survey of Unbanked and Underbanked Households." Washington, DC: Federal Deposit Insurance Corporation.

Federal Reserve Bank of St. Louis. 2004. "Understanding the Dependence on Paper Checks: A Study of Federal Benefit Check Recipients and the Barriers to Boosting Direct Deposit." Washington, DC: U.S. Department of the Treasury Financial Management Service.

Kiviat, Barbara. 2010. "Credit Card Companies Get Their Groove Back." *Time Magazine*. The Curious Capitalist. http://curiouscapitalist.blogs.time.com/2010/02/11/credit-card-companies-get-their-groove-back.

Kuttner, Hans. 2011. "The Move to Digital Payment: When the Check Is No Longer in the Mail." Washington, DC: The Hudson Institute.

Perez, William. 2010. "Tax Preparation Prices and Fees: What's a Reasonable Price to Pay for Preparing Tax Returns?" *Tax Planning: U.S.* About.com. http://taxes.about.com/od/findataxpreparer/a/prices.htm.

Theodos, Brett, Rachel Brash, Jessica Compton, Karen Masken, Nancy Pindus, and C. Eugene Steuerle. 2010. "Characteristics of Users of Refund Anticipation Loans and Refund Anticipation Checks." Washington, DC: U.S. Department of Treasury.

Theodos, Brett, C. Eugene Steuerle, and Jessica Compton. 2011. "Understanding the Demand for High-Cost Tax Advances." Washington, DC: The Urban Institute.

UAA Clearinghouse. 2010. "UAA Suppression Overview." http://www.uaaclearinghouse.com/uaaoverview.aspx.

U.S. Department of the Treasury. 2010a. "Treasury Extends Direct Deposit to Millions of Americans, Phasing Out Paper Checks for Federal Benefit Payments." Washington, DC: U.S. Department of the Treasury, Financial Management Service. http://www.fms.treas.gov/news/press/electronic_benefits_rule.html.

———. 2010b. "Financial Management Service Privacy Act of 1974, as Amended; System of Records." Federal Register 75:241 (December 16, 2010) p. 78802–78804.

U.S. Department of the Treasury, 2011. Unpublished information provided by the Financial Management Service.

U.S. Government Accountability Office. 2011. "2011 Tax Filing: Processing Gains, but Taxpayer Assistance Could Be Enhanced by More Self-Service Tools." Draft Report to Congressional Requesters. GAO-12-176. Washington, DC: U.S. Government Accountability Office.

Woosley, Ben. 2007. "Credit Card Industry and Personal Debt Statistics (2005 and Prior)." CreditCards.com. http://www.creditcards.com/credit-card-news/credit-card-statistics-2005-prior-1276.php.

Wu, Chi Chi, and Jean Ann Fox. 2011. "End of the Rapid Rip-Off: An Epilogue for Quickie Tax Loans." NCLC/CFA 2011 Refund Anticipation Loan Report. Washington, DC: National Consumer Law Center and Consumer Federation of America.

X. Appendix A: Empirical Model and Tables

Using card take-up as an example, the regression model takes the following form:

$$Y_{iz} = \alpha + \beta_1 S_{iz} + \beta_2 F_{iz} + \beta_3 M_{iz} + \delta_1 G_{iz} + \delta_2 X_{iz} + \delta_3 Z_z + v_{iz}.$$

In this model, Y_{iz} indicates whether person i who lives in zip code z applied to receive the *MyAccountCard* (Y_{iz}=1) or did not apply to receive the *MyAccountCard* (Y_{iz}=0). Among the explanatory variables, F_{iz} identifies if person i who lives in zip code z received a card offer with a monthly fee (F_{iz}=1) or without a monthly fee (F_{iz}=0). Similarly, S_{iz} identifies people who received offers with a linked savings account and M_{iz} identifies people who received offers with safety (versus convenience) messaging. The coefficient β_1, for example, identifies the effect of receiving an offer with a monthly fee versus no monthly fee on the likelihood of applying for the *MyAccountCard*.

Beyond the treatment variables, G_{iz} identifies whether the pilot participant was in the second mailing group (letter mailed on February 4, 2011) versus the first mailing group (letter mailed on January 18, 2011). X_{iz} represents individual- and household-level characteristics (e.g., age, race/ethnicity, and income), Z_z represents zip code–level characteristics (e.g., number of free ATMs and percentage of tax returns receiving the EITC), and v_{iz} is the error term.

Table 1: *MyAccountCard* Outcome Measures

Variable	Description
Card Application and Issuance	
Card application	Applied for *MyAccountCard*; applications were accepted through April 30, 2011
Card issuance	Issued a *MyAccountCard*
Card Use	
Card used ever	Any card activity (e.g., deposits, withdrawals) by July 31, 2011; activity from checking authorization of the card account is not considered account use
Card used at least 50% of months	Card used at least 50 percent of months since card issued
Percent of months card used	Percent of months card used out of months since card issued
Card used in last month	Any card activity in the last month examined (July 2011)
Direct Deposits into Card Account	
Tax refund deposited	Federal or state tax refund directly deposited into card account
Other direct deposit ever	Other direct deposit into card account (e.g., earnings from an employer or government benefits) by July 31, 2011
Other direct deposit in last month	Other direct deposit into card account in the last month examined (July 2011)
Card Account Balances	
Average account balance	Average monthly balance (transaction plus savings accounts) across months since card first used[a]
Account balance in last month	Monthly balance (transaction plus savings accounts) in the last month examined (July 2011)[a]
Card Account Fees	
Average variable fees	Average of the monthly variable fees (excludes monthly maintenance fee) across the months card used[b]
Fees in last month	Total fees in the last month examined (July 2011)
Variable fees in last month	Variable fees in the last month examined (July 2011)[b]
ATM fees in last month	ATM withdrawal fees in the last month examined (July 2011)
Card Account Management	
Online account used ever	Logged into online account by July 31, 2011
Text messaging used ever	Text messages pushed or pulled by July 31, 2011

a. The monthly card account balance is the sum of the lowest transaction account balance and the end of month savings account balance.
b. The variable fees are: out-of-network ATM cash withdrawal fee ($2.50), out-of-network ATM balance inquiry fee ($0.50), second card fee ($4.95), FedEx fee ($19.95), lost or stolen card fee ($4.95), foreign transaction fee (3% of transaction amount), teller cash withdrawal fee ($2.50), and fee for in-person deposits at participating retail locations (up to $4.95).

Table 2: Characteristics of *MyAccountCard* Pilot Participants, by Treatment Group

	All	Monthly Fee		Savings Account		Messaging	
		Yes	No	Yes	No	Safety	Convenience
Individual Characteristics							
Age	45.8	45.8	45.8	45.8	45.8	45.8	45.8
Race/Ethnicity							
White	50.1%	50.1%	50.1%	50.1%	50.1%	50.1%	50.1%
Black	30.9%	30.9%	31.0%	31.0%	31.0%	31.0%	31.0%
Hispanic	16.1%	16.1%	16.0%	16.0%	16.1%	16.1%	16.0%
Asian	1.9%	1.9%	1.8%	1.9%	1.9%	1.9%	1.9%
Other	1.0%	1.0%	1.0%	1.0%	1.0%	1.0%	1.0%
Female	51.5%	51.5%	51.6%	51.6%	51.6%	51.6%	51.5%
Household Characteristics							
Children present	15.1%	15.1%	15.1%	15.1%	15.1%	15.1%	15.1%
Income							
<$15,000	37.2%	37.1%	37.2%	37.1%	37.2%	37.2%	37.1%
$15,000–$24,999	28.7%	28.7%	28.7%	28.7%	28.6%	28.6%	28.7%
$25,000–$34,999	34.2%	34.2%	34.2%	34.2%	34.2%	34.2%	34.1%
Underbanked score[a]	5.27	5.28	5.28	5.28	5.27	5.28	5.27
Zip Code–Level Characteristics							
Ease and Cost of Use							
Number of card reload locations	4.68	4.68	4.68	4.69	4.67 *	4.68	4.67
Number of free ATMs	1.48	1.49	1.48	1.48	1.48	1.49	1.48
Tax Return Data							
Received EITC	28.5%	28.5%	28.5%	28.5%	28.5% **	28.5%	28.5% *
Received student loan interest deduction	6.0%	6.0%	6.0%	6.0%	6.0% *	6.0%	6.0%
Filed by third party	61.3%	61.3%	61.3%	61.2%	61.3% **	61.2%	61.3% **
Filed with an ITIN	2.4%	2.4%	2.4%	2.4%	2.4%	2.4%	2.3% *
Urbanicity							
Rural	39.2%	39.2%	39.2%	39.2%	39.2%	39.2%	39.2%
Suburban	22.1%	22.1%	22.1%	22.2%	22.1%	22.2%	22.0%
Urban	24.5%	24.5%	24.5%	24.5%	24.5%	24.5%	24.5%
Observations	808,099	404,085	404,014	404,061	404,038	403,840	404,259

a. The underbanked score is a number between 1 and 9, where a value of 1 indicates households most likely to be unbanked/underbanked and successively higher values indicate a lower likelihood of being unbanked/underbanked.
* denotes significant difference at the 5% level and ** denotes significant difference at the 1% level

Table 3: Characteristics of *MyAccountCard* Cardholders, by Treatment Group

	All	Monthly Fee		Savings Account		Messaging	
		Yes	No	Yes	No	Safety	Convenience
Individual Characteristics							
Age	42.6	42.9	42.3	42.3	42.8	42.7	42.4
Race/Ethnicity							
White	42.1%	40.1%	43.3%	41.0%	43.2%	40.3%	43.8%
Black	47.7%	49.6%	46.7%	47.9%	47.5%	49.7%	45.8%
Hispanic	8.8%	9.6%	8.2%	9.6%	7.8%	8.5%	9.0%
Asian	0.6%	0.3%	0.9%	0.5%	0.8%	1.0%	0.3%
Other	0.8%	0.4%	1.0%	0.9%	0.7%	0.5%	1.1%
Female	60.3%	64.1%	58.1% *	59.5%	61.1%	61.9%	58.7%
Household Characteristics							
Children present	19.4%	18.8%	19.7%	19.3%	19.5%	18.1%	20.6%
Income							
<$15,000	41.4%	40.2%	42.1%	42.2%	40.5%	41.7%	41.1%
$15,000–$24,999	27.6%	30.1%	26.2%	25.9%	29.4%	28.7%	26.6%
$25,000–$34,999	31.0%	29.7%	31.7%	31.9%	30.1%	29.7%	32.3%
Underbanked score[a]	4.07	3.86	4.19 **	3.99	4.15	4.06	4.08
Zip Code–Level Characteristics							
Ease and Cost of Use							
Number of card reload locations	4.44	4.40	4.47	4.51	4.38	4.47	4.41
Number of free ATMs	1.59	1.60	1.58	1.65	1.52	1.56	1.62
Tax Return Data							
Received EITC	30.9%	31.6%	30.4% *	31.1%	30.6%	30.9%	30.8%
Received student loan interest deduction	5.9%	5.8%	6.0%	6.0%	5.9%	5.9%	6.0%
Filed by third party	61.3%	61.5%	61.1%	61.3%	61.2%	61.3%	61.2%
Filed with an ITIN	1.9%	2.1%	1.8%	1.9%	2.0%	1.9%	2.0%
Urbanicity							
Rural	34.6%	34.9%	34.4%	34.9%	34.2%	34.1%	35.1%
Suburban	23.1%	22.2%	23.7%	23.6%	22.6%	23.7%	22.6%
Urban	25.3%	25.8%	25.0%	25.1%	25.5%	25.1%	25.5%
Observations	1,933	717	1,216	992	941	958	975

a. The underbanked score is a number between 1 and 9, where a value of 1 indicates households most likely to be unbanked/underbanked and successively higher values indicate a lower likelihood of being unbanked/underbanked.
* denotes significant difference at the 5% level and ** denotes significant difference at the 1% level

Table 4: *MyAccountCard* Application and Use by Cardholder Status

	All Pilot Participants	Expected Pilot Offer Recipients	Cardholders	Active Cardholders
Card Application and Issuance				
Card application	0.24%	0.28%	--	--
Card issuance	0.24%	0.27%	--	--
Card Use				
Card used ever	0.08%	0.09%	33%	--
Card used at least 50% of months	0.04%	0.04%	15%	46%
Percent of months card used	0.04%	0.04%	16%	49%
Card used in last month	0.03%	0.03%	12%	37%
Direct Deposits into Card Account				
Tax refund deposited	0.03%	0.04%	16%	48%
Other direct deposit ever	0.04%	0.04%	15%	46%
Other direct deposit in last month	0.01%	0.01%	5%	16%
Card Account Balances				
Average account balance	$0.04	$0.05	$17.16	$51.67
Account balance in last month	$0.02	$0.02	$8.34	$25.12
Card Account Fees[a]				
Average variable fees	$0.00	$0.00	$1.70	$5.11
Fees in last month	$0.00	$0.00	$0.49	$3.89
Variable fees in last month	$0.00	$0.00	$0.39	$3.16
ATM fees in last month	$0.00	$0.00	$0.37	$3.01
Card Account Management				
Online account used ever	0.05%	0.06%	22%	43%
Text messaging used ever	0.01%	0.01%	4%	12%
Observations	808,099	707,449	1,933	642

Notes: 808,099 card offers were mailed and an estimated 707,449 card offers were received (based on information from the mail center that received the undelivered letters). The percentages in the "all pilot participants" column are calculated using the number of offers mailed and the percentages in the "expected pilot offer recipients" column are calculated using the estimated number of offers received. The "cardholder" sample includes pilot participants who were issued *MyAccountCards* and the "active cardholder" sample includes pilot participants who used their cards by July 31, 2011.

a. Card Account fees for July are calculated among the subset of active cardholders who used the card in that month (37 percent).

Table 5: The Relationship between Alternative *MyAccountCard* Offers and Card Application and Use

	Monthly Fee (vs. no fee)		Linked Savings Account (vs. no savings account)		Safety Messaging (vs. convenience messaging)	
	All Participants	Cardholders	All Participants	Cardholders	All Participants	Cardholders
Card Application and Issuance						
Card application	-42% **	--	7%	--	-1%	--
Card issuance	-43% **	--	6%	--	-2%	--
Card Use						
Card used ever	-47% **	-8%	-4%	-8%	1%	3%
Used at least 50% of months	-52% **	-14%	-24% *	-27% **	-11%	-7%
Percent of months card used	-50% **	-15% *	-14%	-17% *	-4%	-2%
Card used in last month	-55% **	-20%	-28% *	-30% **	-13%	-10%
Direct Deposits into Card Account						
Tax refund deposited ever	-52% **	-15%	-10%	-15%	5%	8%
Other direct deposit ever	-38% **	5%	-5%	-9%	-9%	-7%
Other direct deposit in last month	-44% **	-5%	-28%	-31%	4%	8%
Card Account Balances						
Average account balance	-$0.05 **	-$14.9 *	-$0.02	-$8.48	-$0.01	-$4.16
Account balance in last month	-$0.04 **	-$12.27 *	-$0.01	-$3.20	-$0.01	-$2.28
Card Account Fees						
Average variable fees	-$0.00 **	$0.16	-$0.00	-$0.09	-$0.00	-$0.06
Fees in last month	-$0.00	$0.28 *	-$0.00	-$0.11	-$0.00	-$0.00
Variable fees in last month	-$0.00	-$0.00	-$0.00	-$0.09	$0.00	$0.03
ATM fees in last month	-$0.00	$0.02	-$0.00	-$0.09	$0.00	$0.04
Card Account Management						
Online account used ever	-55% **	-20% *	2%	-2%	20%	26% **
Text messaging used ever	-63% **	-38% *	16%	8%	0%	6%

Notes: Each row presents results from two separate regression models—one regression for the full sample of pilot participants and a second regression for the subset of *MyAccountCard* cardholders. The models also include controls for mail group (January 18th versus February 4th), age, race/ethnicity, gender, presence of a child in the household, income, underbanked score, number of card reload locations in zip code, number of free ATMs in zip code, rural/suburban/urban location, and zip code-level tax data (percentage who received the EITC, percentage who received the student loan deduction, percentage who used a paid preparer, percentage who used an ITIN).
* denotes significant difference at the 5% level and ** denotes significant difference at the 1% level

Table A-1: Impact of Alternative *MyAccountCard* Offers on Card Issuance, Card Use, and Tax Refund Deposits (Full Set of Probit Coefficients)

	All Pilot Participants		
	Card Issuance	Card Used Ever	Tax Refund Deposited
Treatment			
Monthly fee (vs. no fee)	-0.174 **	-0.180 **	-0.196 **
	[0.015]	[0.024]	[0.034]
Savings account (vs. no savings)	0.018	-0.011	-0.030
	[0.015]	[0.024]	[0.032]
Safety messaging (vs. convenience)	-0.005	0.002	0.012
	[0.015]	[0.024]	[0.032]
Timing of Mailing			
February mailing (vs. January)	-0.134 **	-0.188 **	-0.261 **
	[0.021]	[0.035]	[0.053]
Individual Characteristics			
Age (omitted: age 65 plus)			
Age 19-24	0.301 **	0.345 **	0.542 **
	[0.046]	[0.082]	[0.127]
Age 25-34	0.234 **	0.361 **	0.476 **
	[0.039]	[0.071]	[0.118]
Age 35-44	0.222 **	0.329 **	0.466 **
	[0.038]	[0.071]	[0.117]
Age 45-54	0.255 **	0.342 **	0.470 **
	[0.037]	[0.070]	[0.116]
Age 55-64	0.211 **	0.244 **	0.379 **
	[0.039]	[0.074]	[0.120]
Race/Ethnicity (omitted: White)			
Black	0.105 **	0.0483	0.053
	[0.019]	[0.031]	[0.042]
Hispanic	-0.163 **	-0.201 **	-0.179 **
	[0.028]	[0.049]	[0.069]
Asian	-0.281 **	-0.272	-0.254
	[0.087]	[0.139]	[0.189]
Other	-0.0476	-0.004	0.022
	[0.083]	[0.122]	[0.163]
Female	0.074 **	0.130 **	0.138 **
	[0.016]	[0.025]	[0.035]
Household Characteristics			
Children present	0.049 *	0.083 **	0.065
	[0.021]	[0.031]	[0.043]
Income (omitted: $25,000-$34,999)			
<$15,000	0.034	-0.008	-0.006
	[0.018]	[0.029]	[0.039]
$15,000-$24,999	0.012	0.024	-0.012
	[0.019]	[0.030]	[0.041]
Underbanked score[a]	-0.045 **	-0.042 **	-0.029 **
	[0.003]	[0.005]	[0.007]

(continued on next page)

Table A-1 (continued): Impact of Alternative *MyAccountCard* Offers on Card Issuance, Card Use, and Tax Refund Deposits (Full Set of Probit Coefficients)

	All Pilot Participants		
	Card Issuance	Card Used Ever	Tax Refund Deposited
Zip Code Level Characteristics			
Ease and Cost of Use			
Number of card reload locations	-0.002	-0.005	-0.005
	[0.002]	[0.003]	[0.004]
Number of free ATM's	0.004	0.004	0.008
	[0.003]	[0.005]	[0.006]
Tax Return Data			
Received EITC	0.266 **	0.139	-0.008
	[0.096]	[0.153]	[0.213]
Received student loan interest deduction	1.189 **	0.686	0.700
	[0.391]	[0.610]	[0.815]
Filed by third party	0.360 **	0.142	-0.047
	[0.101]	[0.158]	[0.216]
Filed with an ITIN	-0.522	-0.980	-0.647
	[0.276]	[0.485]	[0.711]
Urbanicity (omitted: urban)			
Rural	-0.036	0.0356	0.086 *
	[0.020]	[0.031]	[0.042]
Suburban	0.011	0.013	-0.038
	[0.020]	[0.033]	[0.048]
Constant	-3.333 **	-3.570 **	-3.833 **
	[0.093]	[0.151]	[0.216]
Observations	808,099	808,099	808,099

a. The underbanked score is a number between 1 and 9, where a value of 1 indicates households that are the most likely to be unbanked/underbanked and successively higher values indicate a lower likelihood of being unbanked/underbanked.
* denotes significant difference at the 5% level and ** denotes significant difference at the 1% level. Standard errors are in brackets

XI. Appendix B: Project Costs

The final costs to the Treasury Department depend in large part on the final number of mailings, enrollments, and card usage levels. The fees payable by Treasury to Bonneville Bank are:

- $.80 for each mail solicitation sent.
- $1.50 for account opening and card issuance fulfillment.
- For card accounts with no monthly fee, $5.95 per month for every active card that does not load at least $1,000 to the card account or initiate 30 purchase transactions in that monthly billing cycle.
- For card accounts with $4.95 Monthly Fee, $1.00 per month for every active card that does not load at least $1,000 to the card account or initiate 30 purchase transactions in that monthly billing cycle.

In addition, there are fees that are not dependent on number of mailings or enrollment and card usage levels:

- Contract with Urban Institute for evaluation of pilot program design and execution - $300,000.
- Reimbursement of up to $650,000 to the Federal Reserve Bank of St. Louis for Web site development, research and marketing support. The Federal Reserve Bank of St. Louis is a Treasury fiscal agent for the purposes of Electronic Funds Transfer operations and marketing strategy.
- Reimbursement to Bonneville Bank for the actual costs up to but not to exceed $45,000 associated with acquiring and developing a mailing list for the pilot.
- $25,000 paid to Bonneville Bank upon successful issuance of all direct mail solicitations.
- $25,000 paid to Bonneville Bank upon the earlier of completion of the pilot evaluation or June 30, 2011.

As of January 2012, the cost of the pilot has been $1,366,081.05 (See table below). The final cost of the pilot will increase slightly as the account cards in circulation continue to be used by customers for the duration of the program.

Actual Tax Time Acount Pilot Program Cost as of January 20, 2012

Payment to Bonneville Bank	$	595,081.05
Payment Urban Institute	$	300,000.00
Payment to Federal Reserve Bank of St Louis	$	471,000.00
Total	$	1,366,081.05

www.ingramcontent.com/pod-product-compliance
Lightning Source LLC
Chambersburg PA
CBHW052020280526
45793CB00005B/1052